Original title:
In the Wake of the Waves

Copyright © 2025 Creative Arts Management OÜ
All rights reserved.

Author: Dorian Ashford
ISBN HARDBACK: 978-1-80581-593-8
ISBN PAPERBACK: 978-1-80581-120-6
ISBN EBOOK: 978-1-80581-593-8

Waters that Remember

Splash and giggle from the tide,
Seaweed hats that no fish hide.
Salty splashes, laughter high,
Crabs tap dance as seagulls fly.

Old boots drift alongside dreams,
Float on stories, crazy schemes.
Jellyfish with jelly brains,
Swim in circles, take the reins.

Horizon of Hope

Waves that whisper jokes to shore,
Sunsets painting tales galore.
Surfers tumble, oh what fun,
Salted hair shines in the sun.

Sandcastles, tall with pride,
Pirate ships that do not hide.
Seashells giggle, oh so bright,
Bring the laughter, day and night.

The Fisherman's Heart

Rod and reel with a twisty hook,
Fish tell tales in every nook.
Maggots wiggle, not a care,
While fishermen knit stories rare.

Caught one fish, but it was a shoe,
Told his friends it's a whale, who knew?
Dreams of halibut, big and wide,
He catches fun, with joy and pride.

Entwined in Ebb and Flow

The tide rushes with a cheeky grin,
Footprints vanish, wave wins again.
Starfish laugh on sandy chairs,
While sea turtles spin in pairs.

Bubbles rise with a joyful cheer,
As dolphins dance, far and near.
Ebb and flow, a silly tease,
Nature's joke in the gentle breeze.

Secrets Beneath the Foam

Bubbles rise, secrets crawl,
Fish in tuxedos having a ball.
Crabs play tag, but who'll tell?
Seaweed sways like a jelly bell.

Octopuses juggling sea shells,
Turtles gossiping, casting spells.
Seahorses dance in a waltz so fine,
All reveling in the ocean's brine.

Sky and Sea Collide

A surfer flops, lands in the drink,
As seagulls laugh, they wink and blink.
Clouds toss sprinkles to liven the show,
While dolphins bust a move, don't you know?

Sunbathers slip, sunscreen flies,
While jellyfish float with glittering ties.
The horizon's a meet-up, a party in blue,
Where sky and sea share a laugh or two.

The Ocean's Heartbeat

The tide's a drummer, with a splashy beat,
Clams clap shells, tapping their feet.
Starfish yawn as the waves parade,
While sea cucumbers don't feel dismayed.

Whales sing tunes in bubbly delight,
As fish swim by, thinking they're light.
Every wave a giggle, every swell a cheer,
The ocean's laughter is crystal clear.

Sheltered by the Tide

Sandcastles rise, the tide's a friend,
While hermit crabs giggle 'round the bend.
Buckets of giggles, shovels of fun,
Under the sun, we frolic and run.

Waves sneak in, wearing frothy hats,
Tickling the toes of curious cats.
Seashells whisper their tales at night,
As the moon smirks, all's cozy and right.

Revelations of the Rising Tide

From the shore I hear a call,
A rubber ducky takes a fall.
Seagulls squawk with cheeky grin,
Stealing fries, their playful sin.

The crabs all dance a jig so fine,
Twirling under the bright sunshine.
Sandcastles bow to royal wave,
As giggles echo, bold and brave.

Dreams Cast adrift

Flip-flops tossed in ocean's embrace,
The tide has taken them to space.
A beach ball's float, a long-lost friend,
Chasing seagulls, the fun won't end.

Drifting dreams on surfboards bright,
Surfing squirrels take to flight.
With laughter loud, the sea does dance,
Each splash a quirk, a hapless prance.

Where Waters Meet the Sky

Clouds like cotton candy swirl,
Children's laughter, joyous twirl.
Kites take off on wind's delight,
Chasing gulls into the night.

A fish with shades, yes, what a sight!
Flapping fins in pure delight.
Wave to dolphins who can't refuse,
To join the party, dancing blues.

Currents of Forgotten Echoes

Old flip-flops float, lost at sea,
Waves giggle loud, oh such glee.
A parrot squawks a pirate's tune,
While beach balls bounce by the moon.

Bubbles rise from toes with flair,
Giggling children without a care.
With every splash, the water sings,
Of memories made, and silly things.

Whispers on the Wind

The seagulls squawk like gossiping friends,
Telling tales as the breeze gently bends.
Sandcastles crumble, a royal decree,
"Not my fault! The tide's got it in for me!"

A crab in a tuxedo waltzes by,
Inviting the shells to a dance, oh my!
With a pinch and a poke, they shimmy and sway,
While the waves laugh and splash, it's a silly ballet.

Shores of Solitude

Where flip-flops fling and sunscreen flies,
A lone beachgoer munches on fries.
The seagulls plot to steal a bite,
"Is that a snack?" they shriek with delight!

A sand dollar rolls by, round and bright,
Challenging seashells to a dance-off tonight.
With shells as judges, the contest begins,
But who will prevail, the seagull with wins?

Fragments of the Sea

A bottle of soda, bobbing away,
Is this treasure or just a display?
Mermaids giggle as they splash and chirp,
"Can someone please catch that fizzy old burp?"

Starfish in sunglasses catch some rays,
While fish flip-flop in a cheeky maze.
"Swim faster!" they yell, "We must break free!"
From the clutches of a hungry old sea spree!

Untamed Horizons

The dolphins decide to throw a party,
With confetti made of seaweed, oh so hearty!
The clams clap along with their shells aglow,
As groovy blue crabs steal the show!

But wait! What's that? A fish in a tie,
Doing the cha-cha as the tides pass by.
"Join me, folks! It's a must-see dance,
At the edge of the sea, let's take a chance!"

The Coral's Cry

Beneath the foam, corals sigh,
A clam just laughed, oh my, oh my!
Crabs in tuxedos dance and twirl,
While tiny fish spin in a whirl.

A starfish waits for its big chance,
To join in on the ocean dance.
Seahorses giggle, flip with glee,
Who knew the sea was so funny?

Anemones wave like they're on stage,
With seaweed doing a froggy page.
When dolphins jump, they crack a joke,
Sea turtles chuckle and provoke.

Crab's got jokes that make fish snort,
Gull's remarks, a salty sport.
With every wave, a chuckle sound,
Under the sea, joy does abound.

Forgotten Beaches

There's a beach where sighs turn to giggles,
Forgotten by waves, where seashells wiggles.
An old flip-flop lays on the sand,
It dreams of toes, a cushioned land.

Sandcastles lean like they're sleepy heads,
While beach balls drift on jellyfish beds.
Tanned folks napping, sunburns in sight,
They wake with a jump at a gull's delight.

Old umbrellas bow like they've seen it all,
Pails and shovels stage a playful brawl.
Seagulls gossip, "Did you hear that?"
The tides play tricks, what a funny chat!

But watch out for crabs with their snappy claws,
They'll poke your toes, without a pause.
In this wacky world where the sunbeams twine,
Sometimes forgotten is pure sunshine.

Salty Breaths and Sandy Hopes

Salty breezes whip 'round with flair,
Tickling noses, teasing hair.
Sandy hopes blow like dandelions,
With seaweed woofs, we're all in line!

One seagull squawks, "Who stole my fries?"
The others chortle, no one lies.
Whales sing songs, though they're out of tune,
As jellyfish float with a quirky croon.

Kids dig holes, looking for treasure,
Finding sea glass brings them great pleasure.
A conch shell's boast, "I'm the loudest here!"
Curly tails wiggle in giggles of cheer.

As tides recede, the fun won't halt,
With sandy footprints in a wacky vault.
Everyone's joy dances with the sea,
In this salty land, we float so free.

Skipping Stones and Lost Wishes

Skipping stones with a plop and a splash,
Each one a wish for a big ol' cash.
Frogs leap in, joining the game,
As laughter spills, not one rocks the same.

A lonely rock sinks, scrambles to swim,
While turtles chuckle, they're quiet and prim.
"Where's our lunch?" the fish shout and pout,
Stomachs grumbling in the playful route.

Wish I could bounce like that smooth stone,
Sliding on waves, no sight of a phone.
Seashells whisper secrets from afar,
While crabs plan heists under a star.

With every toss, a dream takes flight,
Laughter echoes into the night.
Beneath the twilight's warm embrace,
We find lost wishes in this silly place.

Voices from the Nautical Depths

Bubbles and fish, what a sight,
A crab with a hat, quite a delight.
Giggling seaweed, it's quite absurd,
Whispering secrets, yes, I heard.

Octopus juggling shells with flair,
Turtles in sneakers, racing with air.
Starfish calling taxis, wait a bit,
Sandy sea urchins, throwing a fit.

Seagulls debating the best fish fry,
With clam chowder dreams piled up high.
Dolphins on surfboards, catching the breeze,
Sailing the currents, they do it with ease.

So here in the depths, let laughter roll,
With every wave, we share a soul.
For who knew the sea was one big joke,
With all its characters, no need to provoke?

Serenity on the Waters' Edge

The sun sets down, crabs take a stroll,
Seagulls wear shades; they're looking quite droll.
Pelicans gossip about the day's catch,
While fish throw a party, it's quite a match.

Sandcastles built with a silly twist,
Mermaids in flip-flops, you get the gist.
Oysters crafting pearls for a lovely sort,
But clams just complain, they're not the sport.

The breeze tickles boats, they sway with glee,
While barnacles dance, as happy as can be.
With laughter that echoes like waves on the shore,
This water's edge party, oh who could ignore?

So come join the fun, leave worries behind,
As the ocean plays tricks that are one of a kind.
For joy rides the tides, abundant and free,
And all the sea critters just want to be silly.

The Heartbeat of the Harbor

The harbor hums a tune, oh so neat,
With boats doing dances, quite a feat.
Children chase bubbles, dogs bark and leap,
While fish sing along from the depths of the deep.

A lighthouse shines bright, wearing a bow,
Sailboats are prancing, putting on a show.
Seagulls joke loudly, their feathers a-mess,
As they squawk and squabble, oh what a stress.

Docks creak with laughter, in rhythm and rhyme,
The sun sets slowly, mocking the time.
Old sailors chuckle, sharing their tales,
Of whales that stole snacks and snuck on the gales.

So if you hear laughter, and life feels alive,
It's the harbor's heartbeat, a joy to survive.
With each little wave, a chuckle descends,
In this jolly abode, every moment transcends.

Ebb and Flow of Forgotten Dreams

The tide rolls in, with characters strange,
A sockfish lost, oh what a range!
Waves whisper secrets from ages gone by,
While sea cucumbers look up and sigh.

Driftwood with stories, balmy and sweet,
Belly-flopped jellyfish, not quite discreet.
Turtles on surfboards, they're all about style,
Catching the waves with a nonchalant smile.

An octopus poet, pen held with a tentacle,
Writes of adventures, both mundane and magical.
He speaks of lost treasures, and hats made of light,
Of ships that do pirouettes, just out of sight.

So gather your dreams as the tide sweeps them low,
Hold tight to the laughter, let merriment grow.
For even in currents that pull us far away,
The funny remains, like sand on a play.

Moonlit Shores and Silent Roars

Beneath the moon's silvery glow,
Sandy toes dance to and fro.
Crabs all gather for a show,
In moonlight's grip, they steal the flow.

Giggles echo, waves applaud,
To a rhythm that seems quite odd.
Seagulls join with feathery nod,
Stealing snacks from the sunbaked facade.

Flip-flops fly from foot to sea,
While dolphins laugh, "Come join me!"
The tide hums tunes, carefree and free,
As jellyfish juggle, how silly they be!

With starry eyes and jolly cheeks,
The ocean whispers cheeky tweaks.
Floating dreams in watery peaks,
Life's a jest, as laughter sneaks!

Currents of Longing

Waves crash down like playful pups,
Yearning hearts in big, wet cups.
Each splash a giggle, the ocean erupts,
As fish swim by, saying, "What's up?"

Seashells whisper secrets bright,
Of pirate gold and starlit nights.
Yet here we are, our hearts take flight,
Chasing dreams, oh what a sight!

Tides tease with a tickling touch,
Sending us rolling, a little too much.
We laugh as we tumble, not feeling the crunch,
Sipping saltwater from our lunch!

Our hearts float like buoys in the breeze,
Chasing laughter with such silly ease.
In currents of longing, we feel the tease,
For what do we want? Just some seaside cheese!

The Sound of Surrender

Listen close to the ocean's cheer,
Where seagulls caw without a fear.
The tide suggests we shed a tear,
As shells appear, and so do beers!

With every wave, we try to hide,
But our feet are pulled, side to side.
As laughter echoes, we cannot bide,
In salt-kissed dances, old woes abide.

Surfboards tumble, spin, and fall,
Unexpected wipeouts, our favorite call.
With goofy grins, we stand not tall,
In sandy embrace, we answer the squall!

Unruly waves, come play your tricks,
As mermaids offer a few good kicks.
We surrender with laughter, oh what a mix,
In the ocean's grip, it's life's comedy fix!

Seaside Serenity

Sandy castles rise, then crash,
As kids giggle with a splash.
The sun ticks down, a playful stash,
While salty air leaves one bright dash.

Beach balls fly, like fate's little jest,
We chase them down, never to rest.
Laughter mingles, it's simply the best,
In the seaside realm, where joy is blessed.

Umbrellas twirl like hats in a race,
While waves slap knees with friendly grace.
In every grin, there's no trace,
Of worries that time cannot erase.

So come, let's revel in silly delight,
As sea monsters dance in fading light.
With laughter our beacon, shining so bright,
In this serene haven, everything feels right!

Ripples of Remembrance

A seagull squawks at the tide,
While surfers are trying to hide.
With every wave, silly splashes,
They tumble down in funny clashes.

Old crabs dance with a wink,
As beach balls fly and sink.
Each giggle blending with the sea,
Like ocean whispers, wild and free.

A Dance on the Horizon

The sun peeks over the foam,
While dolphins plan their grand roam.
With flips and flops, they bring delight,
Surfing humans run in fright.

A fish in sunglasses swims by,
Passersby let out a sigh.
"Is that a whale or just a boat?"
Turns out it's just a silly goat!

Celestial Blue and Salted Air

Under skies of pastel hue,
Seagulls squabble over stew.
With every wave that rolls in tight,
A splash brings laughter, such a sight!

The starfish wear a fancy hat,
The jellyfish bounces like a brat.
In salty air, we hear the cheer,
Of happy days year after year.

Beneath the Surface

Bubbles rise with a giggle and pop,
While silly fish dance 'til they drop.
"We swim, we glide, we misbehave,"
Chant the fishes in the wave.

A turtle boasts of a big old shell,
While octopuses juggle quite well.
In the ocean, the fun is nonstop,
Where laughter and waves just won't flop!

Island Whispers

On a beach where seagulls dine,
I found a crab who looked divine.
He danced a jig, oh what a sight,
While I just laughed with sheer delight.

A coconut floated by my feet,
Claiming it was the ocean's treat.
I took a bite, it rolled away,
It winked at me, then chose to play.

Laughter echoed down the shore,
As jellyfish began to soar.
They flipped and flopped, what a show,
Like clowns in water, don't you know?

The tide came in with a big splash,
My flip-flops flew—oh what a crash!
Sandy toes and a big wet grin,
The ocean surely likes to win!

Lands Beyond the Breakers

Far away where sea meets sky,
A fish wore glasses, oh my, oh my!
He read a book on how to laugh,
And gave the turtles quite a gaffe.

The crabs held court, with crowns so grand,
Declaring they'd take over the land.
But when they tried to make a run,
They tripped and tumbled—oh what fun!

A parrot spun a silly tale,
Of pirates lost and treasures pale.
Yet when they searched and found a shoe,
They squeaked and squawked, "What shall we do?"

Under the sun, they laughed with glee,
As waves washed in, wild as can be.
Each splash and giggle, a joyful cheer,
In lands beyond, where fun is here!

Harmonies in the Undercurrent

Beneath the waves, a band takes stage,
With sea cucumbers on the page.
They pluck the strings of underwater reeds,
While clownfish gather up the beats.

A sea turtle jived to the tune,
While octopuses had a swoon.
Bubbles floated, making sound,
As sardines swirled 'round and 'round.

The starfish clapped, all five of them,
To joyful songs with no mayhem.
The fish swam by, a colorful crew,
In vibrant hues of red and blue.

The concert ended with a wave,
As seaweed swayed, so brave, so brave.
They laughed and cheered for tides that sway,
In harmonies that lighten the day!

Treasures Among the Pebbles

On a shore of pebbles, shiny and bright,
I found a shell that sparkled in light.
A crab peeked out, said with a grin,
"Don't steal my treasure; I'm hiding within!"

Nearby a rock claimed it was gold,
But really, it just looked old.
The gulls cackled, "What a joke!"
They swooped and dove, oh what a poke!

I gathered stones for a merry band,
Told them we'd form a rock 'n' roll brand.
They rolled around and formed a line,
But one stone said, "I'm not feeling fine!"

The ocean laughed with every swell,
As treasures shined, all thanks to shell.
With every pebble's quirky twirl,
Life's a dance in this splashy swirl!

Beyond the Breakers

Seagulls on surfboards, what a sight,
Catching waves and nibbling on bites.
A crab wears shades, ready to ride,
While fish in tuxedos all glide with pride.

Flip-flops dancing, lost in the foam,
Sandcastles reaching for a sea-salt throne.
The tides are laughing, life's a wacky race,
Where jellyfish boogie and octopuses chase.

Beach balls bouncing, a dog's in the fray,
Chasing his tail while kids laugh and play.
Mermaids sunbathe, sipping on drinks,
Their laughter echoes, causing us to think.

So grab your floaties, join the parade,
Surf's up, who cares if you've made the grade?
Life's too short to take it too slow,
In this watery dance, let your worries go.

Drift of Time

The clock ticks slowly on the beach,
As waves play hopscotch, just out of reach.
Seashells whisper secrets, ancient and weird,
While a sand crab freestyles, clapping is cheered.

Time drifts like a buoy lost at sea,
Seagull squawking, 'Hey, look at me!'
Sunscreen fiascos, oops, what a scene,
With more white on noses than a ghostly sheen.

Kites dancing high, tangled in laughter,
A flip-flop mishap, the dog's running faster.
Sandals and flip-flops take a wild flight,
While kids build castles, so grand and bright.

Tick-tock goes life in a salty ballet,
Time's just a wave, moving, come what may.
Catch it or miss it, we're all on display,
So let's drift through the fun, come join our way!

Living in Fluidity

Waves chatter like gossiping friends,
Swirling together, where fun never ends.
A dolphin does the worm, quite a delight,
While a sea turtle shows off its height.

Life's a cocktail, shaken not stirred,
With seaweed dancing, who needs a word?
The ocean winks, whispering lullabies,
As funky fish flaunt their bright, silly ties.

Surfboards whiz by, in a splashy parade,
Where jellybeans bounce and piñatas are made.
A treasure map made with candy and cheer,
Who needs riches when laughter's so near?

Waves frolic freely, causing a stir,
With laughter and joy, we happily purr.
Embrace the silly in this watery spree,
For we're living in fluidity, wild and free!

Currents of the Past

Once I rode a dolphin strict,
It tossed me like a rubber brick.
I landed on a seaweed bed,
And dreamed of fish instead of bread.

Seagulls laughed, they flew so high,
While I was caught in salty pie.
The crab tried pinching just for fun,
But I outran him in the sun.

Old boots washed up, they tell a tale,
Of sailors lost who drank too pale.
A map to treasure? Just more trash,
My ship's a bottle, oh what a clash!

So here I float, a buoy of glee,
With jellyfish as friends, you see.
We'll dance atop this ocean floor,
And giggle 'til we can't anymore.

Tidepool Tales

In tidepools deep, a crab wore pants,
He danced around and took his chance.
With periwinkles joining in,
They formed a band, just for the win.

Starfish sang with floppy voices,
While sea cucumbers made bad choices.
A clamshell shouted, 'Let's go play!'
But sea urchins said, 'Not today!'

An octopus in shades of green,
Said, 'Watch me turn into a queen!'
He twirled and twisted, oh so grand,
A royal show in the wet sand.

And when the tide began to creep,
The creatures laughed and took a leap.
Back to the depths, they swam with grace,
Till the next party, at their favorite place.

The Color of Water

They say the ocean's blue and bright,
But I once saw it turn to light,
Like lemonade, so sweet and nice,
I nearly jumped in, thought I'd roll the dice.

With every wave came a splashy roar,
A fish wearing glasses begged for more.
'Just a sip!' he yelled through the foam,
'Come join the school, forget your home!'

I swam with dolphins, quite a sight,
They were giggling, full of delight.
But then they fled from a floating shoe,
I swear they laughed as they bid adieu.

So here I sit, on a sandy throne,
With seaweed fries and a seashell phone.
The color of water? A mystery sprawl,
Especially when you leave your drink by the wall.

Echoing Lullabies

The waves sing softly, like a grin,
While starfish hum a silly din.
The sea turtle yawns with a winky eye,
'Time to rest, hear the lullaby.'

Seashells clink like tiny bells,
They carry stories, oh so swell.
A whale's low tune roams the deep,
As fish parade and giggle, leap.

A plankton float with a twinkling sound,
Invited plankton all around.
They danced beneath the moonlit wave,
And found the rhythm that they crave.

So close your eyes, dear ocean friend,
The waves will sing, the night won't end.
As every ripple shares a song,
In the deep blue where we belong.

Footprints in the Waking Tide

Sandy prints that lead nowhere,
Dancing crabs, they stop and stare.
Flip-flops flying, I laugh and squeal,
As seagulls plot their next big meal.

The ocean giggles, waves in a rush,
Splashing my toes with a playful hush.
I trip and tumble, arms flail wide,
A comical plunge, oh silly pride!

With every splash, a giggle grows,
A fish in a bottle says, 'Here it goes!'
My hat takes flight, a seagull's delight,
Chasing my laughter, in pure starlight.

And as I rise, all drenched and spry,
I find my footprints, now a sly lie.
The tide moves on, it's clear to see,
The silly journey was just for me!

Driftwood Chronicles

A piece of wood with tales to tell,
It caught a ride on the ocean swell.
Balancing hopes on its weathered back,
While clam diggers plot their next snack.

I named it Jasper, a noble drift,
Half-sunk in seas, discovering gift.
"What's the plan?" I slyly asked,
It only sighed, a thoughtless task.

A crab scuttled past, waving hello,
Jasper just chuckled, 'I'm on with the flow.'
"Why rush?" he quipped, "The tide's got our change,
Just kick back, relax, this sea's quite strange."

And there I sat, with driftwood so wise,
We swapped silly thoughts under sunny skies.
Just me and my dreams, a wood and a breeze,
The ocean laughed, put my mind at ease.

Memories in the Salt-Kissed Air

With a surge of giggles, I take a dive,
Jumping the waves, feeling so alive.
A jellyfish wobbles, trying to flee,
While I invent stories for him and me.

Salt-kissed hair, like tangled vines,
I dance with seagulls, making designs.
The air is filled with laughter and glee,
As crabs throw confetti, oh what a spree!

Shells whisper secrets of days gone by,
"Was that a dolphin? Nope, just a shy guy!"
Each gust of wind carries tales anew,
Of flip-flop fiascos and oceanic coups.

Yet as the sun sets, with hues so bright,
I ponder the day, a comic delight.
Memories linger, like sand in my shoes,
In the salt-kissed air, I'll never lose.

The Pulse of the Coastal Breeze

A gentle breeze tickles my nose,
It swirls around like it surely knows.
It whispers jokes of days gone past,
"Why worry, my friend? Just have a blast!"

Sandcastles rise, then tumble with style,
Each grain a giggle, each wave a smile.
The breeze gives chase to a runaway hat,
While children point, and we both laugh at that.

Oh, the surfers glide like feathers in air,
While I trip over my own toes with flair.
"Catch me if you can!" the breeze seems to sing,
While I tumble again, oh what joy it brings!

With every laugh, the sun sinks down,
Casting shadows, and my worries drown.
A dance of delight, with the ocean's tease,
I simply float on the pulse of the breeze.

Driftwood Dreams

A piece of wood with stories to tell,
It floated by like a wayward shell.
I gave it a hat and a grin so wide,
Now it's my friend on this seaside ride.

We built a throne on the sandy shore,
Where crusty crabs dance and seagulls roar.
A castle made of driftwood and sand,
With snack time rules that never were planned.

As the tide rolls in, our thoughts take flight,
Ballets of fish twirl in the moonlight.
We laugh at the waves that splash on our toes,
For driftwood dreams are the best kind of prose.

With seaweed crowns, we reign and prance,
Our royal court is a mermaid dance.
In the ocean's embrace, we'll twirl and spin,
For driftwood and dreams are a winner's win.

Beneath the Sail

A shipyard cat with a pirate's flair,
Swipes my sandwich without a care.
He's got a patch, a telescope too,
Sailing the seas in his dreams of stew.

The wind tickles chins with a cheeky blow,
While gulls plot schemes from the rigging below.
'This fish is fresh!' they holler and dive,
A buffet of laughter keeps us alive.

With biscuits and cheese, we anchor in fun,
The sun sets low, and the day is done.
Under the stars, a tale we'll weave,
Of misplaced sails and a cat who believes.

The water may rock as the night drifts in,
But our hearts are light with a giggly grin.
For under this sail, we've nothing to fear,
Just whispers of mischief, and a whole lot of cheer.

Whispers of the Ocean

The ocean talks in splashes and sighs,
With tickling waves and surprise replies.
'Why do fish wear scales?' I ask, bemused,
'To impress the prawns at the seafloor's blues!'

A jellyfish wobbles, a light show twist,
While crabs do the cha-cha, a dance with a twist.
I clap my hands as they shimmy about,
A crustacean cabaret with giggles and clout.

We chat with sea turtles, wise and slow,
'What's the key to happiness? Don't go with the flow!'
They wink as they drift through the bubbles of fun,
A party of sea life, oh how we've won!

So let the waves whisper, let the tide roar,
With laughter as my compass, I'll explore.
In the salty breeze, we'll dance through the night,
With whispers of joy that shine ever bright.

Chasing Seagulls at Dusk

We race the seagulls, they flutter and swoop,
Laughing out loud, we jump through the hoop.
Their wings flap wildly, a feathery spree,
While I do my best to run like the sea.

The sunset paints colors, a canvas so grand,
While gulls play hide and seek on the sand.
I do a quick shuffle, then trip on a shell,
And join the seagulls in a giggly yell.

They tease me for sneakers, so clumsy and bright,
While I laugh at their antics, soaring in flight.
With popcorn to share, we end our chase,
These feathered companions know how to embrace.

As twilight wraps all in a cozy hue,
With the whispers of waves, our friendship grew.
So here's to the seagulls, my partners in crime,
Chasing the sunset, just wasting some time.

Nautical Nostalgia

Once a sailor, bold and spry,
Lost my hat, oh my, oh my!
Chased it down with all my might,
Waved goodbye to the seagull's flight.

Riding waves on my old boat,
Tried to steer while stuck in gloat.
The fish laughed as I took a dive,
Guess that's how I feel alive!

Old tales told of mermaids fair,
But I think I saw a teddy bear.
He was dancing on the prow,
Said he'd sail with me right now!

With a grin, we sailed away,
Me and my bear, come what may.
We'll fish for socks and sing some tunes,
A pirate crew with silver spoons!

Currents of Change

The tide rolls in, takes my shoe,
Waves of chaos, what to do?
I shout to fish that swim so fast,
'Hey, come back, my shoe's a blast!'

My boat's a math whiz, can you believe?
Translating waves, but still we grieve.
For every wave that splashes high,
I ponder why my cookies fly!

Change is here, the gulls agree,
Skydiving fish, oh could it be?
With every flip and every fluke,
I turn the tide, mind on the spook!

Caught a crab with my bear's old sock,
It pinched me good, oh what a shock!
But laughter echoes through the foam,
On this wild and wavy home.

Beneath the Wake

Underneath the frothy crest,
Fish have parties, a sly jest.
They dance and twirl like grand old pros,
Wearing hats made from seaweed bows.

I peeked down, they waved hello,
With sea cucumbers in tow.
"Join our feast, we've bread and spread!"
I chuckled, "Maybe later, I'll be fed!"

A dolphin flipped, a sight to see,
He threw a fish, said, "Catch with glee!"
Missed the snack, but what a splash,
I'd prefer a fishy mustache!

The underwater life is grand,
With octopuses in a band.
They sing of sailors who come to play,
Guess I'll dive in, bright as day!

The Call of the Sirens

Siren songs from rocks so steep,
Promise treasures rich and deep.
But I drooled over the crusty bread,
Forget the glitter, just feed me instead!

Their voices float, a tempting tune,
I wave back, with a silly swoon.
"Come, good sailor, sail our way!"
But food's my radar, hip, hooray!

With fishy faces, they bend and sway,
"Join our dance!" they sweetly say.
But I'd rather munch on some seaweed chips,
Than dance around with silly flips!

So off I sail, laughter my guide,
Leaving sirens feeling snubbed and fried.
For life's a feast upon the foam,
I'll be the sailor who calls it home!

Journey of the Rising Tide

A crab danced sideways, quite a sight,
He thought he was graceful, but try as he might.
Seagulls chuckled, they flew up high,
What a comical scene beneath the bright sky.

Jellyfish floating, looking quite grand,
With tentacles flailing, they're hard to understand.
They bobbed and they weaved, all over the place,
Like little balloon animals, lacking all grace.

A fish gave a wink, its scales all aglow,
It juggled some seaweed, putting on a show.
The tide rolled in laughter, the waves tossed with glee,
Nature's own circus, for every fish to see.

And when the sun set, the tide took a bow,
As crabs wrapped up their wild, underwater fiesta now.
With giggles and splashes, the creatures conspired,
In the salty soirée, nobody retired.

To Touch the Infinite

The ocean sang lullabies full of cheer,
An octopus waltzed, its limbs wide and near.
It grabbed a seashell, wore it like a hat,
Decorating itself—who knew cephalopods could chat?

Waves tickled the beaches with playful delight,
As starfish performed, twinkling in the light.
Seashells cheered loudly, from under the sand,
They'd all gathered together, part of a band!

A dolphin zipped by, doing flips in the sun,
With a splash and a giggle—it's all just for fun.
"Watch me!" it squeaked, "I'm the coolest of all!"
But it tripped over seaweed and took quite a fall.

As night approached softly, with a twinkling sky,
The waves whispered stories, making time fly.
With laughter of creatures and a wink of the moon,
The ocean's chuckle echoed a merry tune.

The Salt of Memory

A wise old turtle, so slow and so sly,
Recited old tales, a grand reason why.
He spoke of the clams, with pearls inside,
Confessing the truth that they often would hide.

The gulls overhead, held a festival fair,
With spoons in their beaks, they cooked up some air.
"Try the sea breeze spaghetti!" they chirped with a grin,
But as they took bites, they just spat it back in.

An urchin chimed in, with spines all around,
"I'll trade you a memory, I've lost and I've found!
For a splash of that salty, delicious sea foam,
Let's capture the laughter, forever to roam."

And so in the currents, the stories were spun,
With giggles and splashes, the fun had begun.
Each frolicsome wave held a tale in its heart,
In the salt of their memories, they'd never depart.

Waves That Carry

A fish with a bowtie swam in a rush,
It thought it looked dapper, oh such a plush!
But a wave gave a giggle, pushed him to swirl,
And the fish did a flip, just like a whirl.

Crabs formed a party, in the bright, carefree foam,
With disco shells spinning, they turned it to home.
"How do you like dancing?" one crab asked the tide,
With a wink and a nod, the wave replied!

Seashells joined in, with a jig and a jive,
Waves humming along, made the creatures come alive.
"Let's ride on this laughter, we'll sail through the night,
With currents of joy, everything feels right!"

As frothy waves rolled in, the beach came alive,
With bubbles of giggles, they started to thrive.
And just like their dances, forever they'll flow,
In waves full of laughter, where joy steals the show.

Secrets of the Flowing Sea

The crab wears a hat, oh what a sight,
He dances on sand, by the pale moonlight.
Fish play a game, quite oddly they dart,
In a bubble parade, they dance with heart.

The starfish is sassy, with arms spread wide,
Claiming the rock, with nowhere to hide.
An octopus juggles with shells in a show,
While seagulls argue, "Hey, that's my dough!"

A dolphin swims by, with a giggle and splash,
Sneaking up close, for a quick, funny flash.
"Did you hear?" it sings, "I can jump the moon!"
While clams giggle softly – "Oh please, make it soon!"

With laughter and waves, the tale unfolds,
Curious fish, with secrets untold.
They whisper and giggle, beneath bubbles bright,
In the watery world, full of silly delight.

Lullabies from the Briny Depths

The seaweed sways to a bizarre tune,
While mermaids giggle, beneath the full moon.
A fish in pajamas, ready for bed,
Snickers at crabs, who decorate their head.

"Goodnight, little guppy, sleep tight in your bed,
Don't dream of the shark who just wants to be fed!"
The whispers of currents, a soft serenade,
Tickle the sand, as the night masquerade.

The clams hum a lullaby, sweet and low,
While barnacles rock to and fro, to and fro.
A seahorse yawns, in his cozy sea nook,
Daring the jellyfish to read a good book.

With bubbles of giggles, the night slips away,
As snoring sea turtles drift off to play.
In dreams full of laughter, the creatures dive deep,
In the briny depths where the giggles don't sleep.

Reflections of the Moonlit Sea

Under the moon's smile, the tide starts to play,
Fish skate on waves, in a wobbly ballet.
The tides chuckle softly, in ripples and sways,
As squids tell tall tales, of their silliest days.

A seal rides a wave, with a hula-hoop flair,
While clowns at the shore toss their pies in mid-air.
Seagulls do pirouettes, just to impress,
While sardines giggle, in their shiny, slick dress.

The moon winks down, with a mischievous glow,
As laughter erupts from below, "Oh, hello!"
"Catch me if you can!" calls the fish with a wink,
But the tide just replies, "I don't even blink!"

Enchanted by moonbeams, the night's full of fun,
With each wave that crashes, more yarns spun.
In reflections so sweet, life's a playful spree,
With creatures of the dark, in a light hearted glee.

The Song of the Surging Surf

The waves crash and babble, a giggly delight,
Seagulls with top hats, prepare for the night.
Surfboards are whispering secrets of speed,
As fish in sunglasses slip onto their steed.

The bubbles they make, rise up with a cheer,
"Watch out, here comes a fish on a beer!"
They frolic and splash, in a watery ball,
While sea cucumbers join the grand hall.

The tide marches in, with a comical beat,
As sea stars go dancing, right off their cold seat.
A shore crab breaks out in a tap-dance parade,
Spinning and twirling, the beach they invade.

With laughter and waves, the surf sings a tune,
Whistling merrily, love songs to the moon.
In the playful ocean, all life finds a laugh,
Where each splish and splash draws a joyful photograph.

Echoes of the Tides

The crab wore a hat, quite fancy and pink,
He danced on the sand with a wink and a wink.
The seagulls all laughed as he tripped on his shell,
He shouted, "Hey there! Who's the best dancer? Well!"

A fish told a joke, but it flopped in the fry,
The octopus chuckled, "You've got eight arms, why?"
With bubbles he laughed, rolling side to side,
While a clam kept on snoring, blissfully wide-eyed.

The tide rolled in, bringing shells in a race,
While a snail said, "Slow down, I can't keep this pace!"
A dolphin flipped high, caught the sun in a spin,
"You'll never beat me, I'm the tide's only twin!"

At sunset they gathered, a party unique,
With bubbles and laughter, it was never bleak.
The waves whispered stories, all goofy and grand,
As night closed the curtain on this coral band.

Whispers on the Shoreline

A sandcastle stood, proud and tall in the sun,
With a royal flag flapping, he thought it was fun.
Then came the tide, with a cheeky little grin,
Sipping the castle, said, "Let this feast begin!"

A starfish played poker, dealt cards with a flair,
While a clam grumbled, "Hey! That's not really fair!"
The barnacles watched from their stony old place,
As seaweed spun tales of a great ocean race.

The tide whispered tales of the lands far away,
Of mermaids and pirates who danced in the spray.
Then a jellyfish bobbed, looking lost in the fray,
"Can anyone tell me if I'm headed that way?"

The sun dipped low, painting skies in a swirl,
As a crab slid by, with a tap-dancing twirl.
And all of the beach, with its laughter and cheer,
Knew someday it'd rise and bring friends back here!

Beneath the Cresting Foam

A fish in a bowtie swam down for a meal,
Who knew that the sea could have such great appeal?
He shouted, "Oh dear! It's a feast fit for kings!"
While a shrimp in a tux dove in, sprouting wings.

The waves laughed aloud, tickling sand on the land,
As a clam made a crown, using shells close at hand.
With pearls all around, it was quite the display,
The sea critters cheered, what a royal array!

A sea turtle slow wobbled, caught in a groove,
While crabs danced in rhythm, all ready to move.
They formed a conga line, shells clattering with glee,
As a dolphin jumped high, shouting, "Join in with me!"

With a splash and a dash, they swirled in delight,
As the moon cast a glow on this party so bright.
So here's to the foam, waves rolling and free,
Where laughter and joy flow like tides of the sea!

Murmurs of the Deep

A whale kept on singing, with notes low and deep,
While a fish joined along, dreaming dreams in his sleep.
They formed a duet that rippled and swayed,
The ocean a concert where all could be played.

A crab with a microphone shouted, "Can you hear?"
He rapped about barnacles, shedding a tear.
With a splash of the tail, the audience roared,
As a blowfish chimed in, with a tune he adored.

The jellyfish waved, glowing bright in the dark,
While a pufferfish puffed, turning into a shark.
"That's some heavy magic in this underwater show!"
The octopus juggled, putting on a great glow.

As currents grew strong, the night danced in waves,
With pirate fish cheering in their planktonic caves.
So here's to the tunes that the waters convey,
Where laughter and music will never decay!

Stars and Seafoam

The stars started dancing, oh what a sight,
While seafoam twinkled, it shone so bright.
A crab tried to salsa, he lost his way,
Then slipped on a shell, what a clumsy display!

The fish threw a party, with bubbles and cheer,
They all wore their hats, each one quite dear.
A seagull came crashing, mentioned the fun,
But tripped on a wave, said, 'Please, I'm just done!'

The moon joined the laughter, as tides rolled and spun,
While jellyfish jigged, saying, "Aren't we just fun?"
With laughter and splashes, the night took a bow,
A scene so absurd, "Get your cameras now!"

In the depths of the ocean, the jokes overflow,
Where silliness thrives, and the tickles do grow.
As sea turtle grinned, with shells all aglow,
"Who knew underwater could be such a show?"

Fragile Horizons

On the edge of the shore, where horizons meet,
A clam tried to dance, but fell on its feet.
With sand in its shell, it let out a shout,
"Next time I'll wear my best shoes, no doubt!"

The gulls perched above, giggling all day,
As sea stars debated, who'd win the ballet.
"Not you!" said the turtle, "You can't even spin!"
The crowd roared with laughter, let the fun begin!

With a wink and a splash, the waves joined in too,
Creating a rhythm, a dance just for you.
A crab brought a radio, turned it up high,
And all of the sea life began to comply!

They twirled and they spun, a funny old crew,
And the fish rolled their eyes, saying, "What can we do?"

When the sun dipped below, and the day turned to night,
They chuckled and splashed, oh what a delight!

Depths of Discovery

A fish with a hat swam past the old wreck,
He giggled and danced, saying, "What the heck!"
The octopus, posed wearing shades made of glass,
Said, "I'm too cool, you won't catch me fast!"

While undersea researchers floated about,
They missed every signal, just filled with doubt.
A dolphin named Charlie threw bubbles around,
While muttering, "Science, oh what a clown!"

With gadgets and gizmos, they fumbled and fell,
Promising wonders, all crafted too well.
But reality struck in that blue, bumpy ride,
As the fish took the wheel, "Let's go for a glide!"

The depths held their secrets, tucked neatly away,
But laughter and splash made the night turn to day.
So while the explorers were lost in their quest,
The ocean just joked, "Now that's what I jest!"

A Canvas of Blue

On a canvas of blue, the sea splashed around,
With color and laughter, the joy was profound.
The whales rolled their eyes at a dolphin's big dive,
"Who taught you to jump?" they'd ask with a jive!

A seahorse on roller skates zoomed through the brine,
While fish cheered in chorus, "You're doing just fine!"
But a starfish got dizzy, it slipped on its leg,
And landed on corals, what a silly peg!

With bubbles and giggles, the sharks joined the play,
Chasing their tails in a most whimsical way.
"I'm meant to be scary!" a great white complained,
Yet tickled by seaweed, he just laughed and remained.

As the sun set in colors that sparked up delight,
A conch shell piped up, "Time to dance through the night!"
So the ocean kept spinning, with humor on cue,
In a world like no other, a canvas of blue!

The Silence Between the Swells

The ocean sighed, took a break,
Seagulls perched, soaked in cake.
A fish in a hat, quite absurd,
Hoping to catch a glimpse of a bird.

Sunburned crabs doing a dance,
Chasing their shadows, not a chance.
The tide rolled in with a bubble of cheer,
Splashing the beachgoers, oh dear!

A clam gave a wink, quite the flirt,
Whispered to starfish, "You're a nerd!"
The bubbles laughed, left trails of fun,
As the sun dipped low, day's work was done.

Journeying with the Wind and Waves.

The breeze was cheeky, played with the sand,
A surfboard lonely, he had no hand.
Caught in a joke, a wave tipped its hat,
"Surf like the seals, but not like that!"

In a kayak, a squirrel took charge,
Paddling hard, feeling quite large.
Paddle splashes rang like a bell,
Echoing laughter, all went well.

A crab in sunglasses, a true chic trend,
Paddled around, oh, what a friend!
Seashells wiggled to a groovy beat,
Party on the beach, oh, what a treat!

Tides of Reflection

A wave peeked over, gave me a grin,
"Why do they call it a beach when you swim?"
I chuckled back, with a dig and a quip,
"Because if it's deep, it's a ship of a trip!"

The moon grinned down, played peek-a-boo,
Whispered to the seaweed, "Hey, how are you?"
Starfish tossed jokes to jellyfish friends,
Laughter traveled where the shoreline bends.

A dolphin giggled, shared a fishy tale,
Of meetings gone wrong with a clumsy whale.
We all came together, so silly, so bright,
As the tide rolled in, giggles took flight.

Echoes of the Deep

Bubbles burst out, like laughter in air,
A fish with a bow tie, debonair flair.
"Why the outfit?" asked a passing ray,
"To impress the sharks on their special day!"

An octopus juggled, quite the surprise,
Mussels and clams, oh my, what a prize!
A sea cucumber laughed, squished in the fun,
"I'm just here to soak up the sun!"

With each crashing wave, a funny refrain,
The ocean's own stand-up, never mundane.
As the tide's last whisper faded away,
We waved goodbye, the end of the day.

www.ingramcontent.com/pod-product-compliance
Lightning Source LLC
Chambersburg PA
CBHW072134070526
44585CB00016B/1679